THE TRUTH ABOUT SANTA CLAUS:
How Adults Can Join Their Children On The Big Red Knee

by

Apollo Starmule

Apollo Starmule

Apollo Polyhistor Starmule is one of the new breed of "soul geographers", an exponent of the new psychology which is millions of years young. His books are available at online retailers throughout the universe, and at the more conscientious physical bookstores.

This Goode Booke Published By

SATYA YUGA BOOKS ™
Asheville Weaverville Nacogdoches Tokyo

To All Awakened Children

THE TRUTH ABOUT SANTA CLAUS:
How Adults Can Join Their Children
On The Big Red Knee

ISBN 978-0-9763230-3-7

"I value my doctorate and my elf suit equally."--Dr. William Bloom

CHAPTER ONE: To Tell The Truth

Parents have been telling their kids the truth all along about Santa Claus. They just didn't know it.

* * *

I remember being told about the young boy who came home from school, his faith in the world he thought he knew beginning to waver because someone had told him there was no such thing as Santa Claus. So of course he went to his mother for reassurance . . . and she knew the dreaded day had come when she would have to tell him the "truth" that Santa did not exist. As she knocked the foundations out from under his world by this admission, two big tears began slowly to trickle down his cheeks, whereupon the mother herself began to bawl in the agony of her deception, and in the necessity of this admission. The boy moved toward his mother to comfort her, but this was a difficult job, as she knew she had just defeated the vision of goodness most dear to the child's heart. So her agony was more prolonged even than her son's grief at losing his faith in the figure which he had regarded with the type of awe usually reserved for a god.

This event, which is repeated in countless

homes every year, was related to me many years ago by the parental culprit who had destroyed her son's faith in miracles, paving the way for him to lose his faith in the divinity of the earth, and in the perception that would allow him to directly tap into that divinity and experience it firsthand.

When the child was a little younger I had wanted to see whether he remembered his past lives, so I asked him one day, "Do you remember when you were big?" This Caucasian child told me that he did remember when he was big, and that he had been a "big black man" and that he had been killed when a tree fell on him in the forest. I think he had been cutting the tree down, but this was years ago and I don't remember for sure. Anyway, it seems likely he or someone would have been cutting it down, as trees seldom fall on a man out of the blue.

This business of manipulating children's faith in the divine, then a few years later of knocking the foundations out from under that faith, has to stop. And it can stop, right here, right now, with you and your loved ones after you've read this tract I've been thoughtful enough to provide you with. For you see, Santa Claus *does* exist, has probably always existed, and always will exist, though we can expect him to change his uniform every few centuries or millennia.

Santa *lives*, and the earth resounds to his

sacred breath, his *breathingness*, every Yuletide season. He just doesn't behave exactly as we've been led to believe by people who are limited by a materialistic consciousness. You can't perceive a divine manifestation thru the lens of materialism; this fact should be obvious to anyone who cares to consider the matter. So what we have to do is to determine how to coax the material world into resonating to the tone of divinity, thus eventually becoming a conscious part of that divinity. Really, the material world is already part of the divine world, because every manifestation in nature is divine. What we have to do is make the material world aware of the gospel, the good news, that it is divine and that its essential nature is divine, so that it will want to cooperate with God.

In fact, the world that we typically regard as the material world is one of the levels of God; you could say that the material world is the outermost level of God. So our job is to make the material world aware of its own nature, and to teach it to reflect that nature, cooperating intimately with all the other levels of God.

Ultimately, God's nature is love, so ultimately the nature of the material world is love, too. And once every molecule of the material world has allowed itself to be permeated with love, it will know itself as

God, and in fact will know itself as Compassion, with human beings having served to help engineer that Compassion which it was always the material world's Destiny to reflect.

CHAPTER TWO: Corps of Engineers

Santa Claus is the head of a vast Corps of Engineers who are responsible for helping attune the earth to the energy of Goodwill, which itself can be considered the "lowest" manifestation of Love. Really, there is no "higher" or "lower" in the Kingdom of Love, but we are hamstrung to some degree by the limitations inherent in language as we try to communicate among ourselves about these things. Perhaps this is why Santa and his Corps usually employ certain sound vibrations in their communications and in influencing the material earth to vibrate to Goodwill, and in encouraging the human heart to begin to sing the tune of Goodwill within itself; not with words, but with an unconditional energy-acceptance of all beings, and of the right of all beings to live free and uncluttered lives sharing the energy of their hearts with those about them.

Santa Claus is an Angel, a Great Being who is both the embodiment and supervisor of the Spirit of Christmas . . . the Spirit of Goodwill. And yes, he often really does appear in a red suit and hat and with a long white beard. Angels don't have the same relation to "literal truth" that human beings do; sometimes I'm not sure they have any relation to "literal truth" at all. Angels know themselves as mythical beings, and they interact with Humanity thru the lens of myth. They absorb Human impressions of Themselves, and they represent themselves to people according to the nature of the impressions they've absorbed. "Telling the truth" from the Angel perspective means accurately representing something in the consciousness of whatever Human they are interacting with. Sometimes the Human will be aware of a particular continuum of impressions in his consciousness, and thus not be surprised when the Angel represents that particular continuum, or some part of that continuum. Other times, the Angel may reflect something the Human wasn't aware he carried in his consciousness, and this can come as quite a surprise.

Angels are also known as "Devas"; the terms are interchangeable and more often than not I find myself using the term "Deva", so let us begin to grow accustomed to the use of this term at this point of our tract.

The Deva Kingdom is composed of the tiniest little nature spirits who will one day evolve into Angels, or fully-fledged Devas, on "up" to Mighty Devas whose natures we cannot begin to fathom, and who rule over solar systems, galaxies and universes. Their keynote is Service; each of these beings, from the little nature spirit whose sole duty is to tend one leaf of a pokeberry bush, on up to those who provide the organizing field that holds together a universe, is intimately involved in resonating to a Pattern of Service. Some would call this telepathy, but this type of resonating to Pattern actually goes far beyond anything human beings typically regard as telepathy--and again, it has little if anything to do with language. Communication thru Patterning occurs in the form of energy-impulses which are not subject to the limitations of words, and it is instantaneous, so Santa knows immediately what is on his elf's mind, and the elf immediately knows Santa's response, and the Pattern shifts accordingly and immediately in a sea of flexibility.

So now you can tell your kids that Santa really does exist, and you can maintain a good conscience all the while. And you will never have to tell them that he does not exist, because his existence is proven by that consciousness that resonates to the energy of Goodwill. I am sure that Santa is tired of being denied, so let's get on with it, shall we?

CHAPTER THREE: Milk and Cookies

I am sure Santa appreciates those families and individuals who leave milk and cookies out for him at Christmas, just as I am sure the dairy and cookie industries appreciate such thoughtfulness. (If you don't support the cultivation of livestock for food, I am sure Santa will be just as pleased if you leave him a glass of soymilk or other vegan alternative.)

But how can Santa be everywhere at once, you ask, as well you might. This is one of the most troubling questions facing modern physicists. If you're taking an upper division physics class, you know what I mean.

Santa both is and is not everywhere at once, honey chile. Let me explain.

First, the energy field we call Goodwill, which Santa is the custodian of, basically *is* everywhere at once and is especially enlivened during the holiday season, both by the efforts of Santa and his Corps and by the efforts of Human Beings who attune themselves to this field of Goodwill. The particular Great Deva we call Santa Claus, who represents Goodwill on this planet, is not exactly everywhere at once, but maintains a certain poise that gives direction and stability to the field of Goodwill, while other Devas of lesser rank actually do most of the fieldwork of Santa . . . they carry his energy, and they dress like him, and they look like him, so they basically *are* him. It is far more convenient than the Great Deva having to do all the work himself . . . which he wouldn't be able to do, anyway, because if he tried the energy field of Goodwill would collapse and chaos would result. He *has* to have a Corps of subordinate Santas, as well as other types of nature spirits, to carry out most of the various aspects of his fieldwork.

There is one Great Santa, and a whole huge network of subordinate Santas, and this is how Santa gets around to every receptive location in one day every year. Of course, he also puts in appearances throughout the year at appropriate moments to those who are receptive to the energy of Goodwill; if you feel the vibration of Goodwill in the air, it is a sign that Santa is there. Anytime Goodwill is born in the human heart, Santa is there, serving as the midwife.

Putting up your Christmas tree can be considered a ritual to invoke Santa, and I have it on good authority that that is how Santa perceives it. Putting out the milk and cookies on Christmas Eve is an additional ritual of invocation, from Santa's viewpoint. These are joyous rituals, and should not be viewed as trivial or thru the lens of materialism if they are to have any positive vibrational effect. It goes without saying that kids view the matter correctly until they are told the lie that Santa doesn't exist. It is very strange that parents first tell kids the truth, then later tell them a lie and represent the lie as some new "truth". Perhaps I am being a little hard on parents; maybe most of them can't help this state of affairs, having been caught in a web of material deceit themselves from the time they were taught that Santa is the Deity of Greed, or that Santa doesn't exist, whichever lie predominated in their homes on the day their faith was destroyed. But now that I have explained the matter to you, there is no more excuse for the emotional/spiritual violence of denial of Goodwill, or of trying to prostitute Goodwill into a stale lust for material objects.

Not that there is anything wrong with children getting toys, mind you. On the contrary, the exchange of gifts at Christmas is felt by children as Goodwill, so the exchange of gifts is an important ritual of invocation. So the toy manufacturers can relax; I'm not going after them in this document.

It is okay to tell kids the truth that parents leave the gifts under the tree, and that Santa comes along in the night and blesses the gifts and deposits the energy of Goodwill which the exchange of gifts represents. And you will probably want to tell them that this energy of Goodwill--of *lovingkindness*--is the reason they are able to enjoy the gifts to begin with, and is the whole reason they are able to enjoy the holiday season. Yes, the release from the public schools for a while is something to be thankful for, but this is kind of a negative release of burdensome tension, rather than a positive embrace of joy. The freedom that comes upon release from public schools is a great wonder to be enjoyed, but it is not nearly as great as the wholesome, abundant joy of Goodwill that comes to the awakened Heart.

And speaking of public schools, they seem to be allowing themselves to degenerate more every year in one way or another, including by denying the existence of Santa Claus. The public schools consider Santa to be a religious figure, and the schools are anti-religious, so they are willing to sacrifice this wholesome energy of Goodwill to their terror of religion. They prefer terror to Love! No wonder so many problems crop up in the schools; the schools are incubators of inhumanity!

Well, Santa *is* a religious figure, but he is also an Angel, and thus is a spiritual figure. I was there in 1776 and in the aftermath of the Revolution, and I don't care what the idiot scholars have to say about the Work we did at that time. Our Work was never meant to deny God! Our Work was never meant to do anything but encourage the spread of Goodwill, not knock it down and try to forget about it.

Yes, Santa supports religion. He supports religion in general, not just Christianity. In fact, in his current guise, he appears to have styled himself after a Norse God, so it would probably be fair to say that in terms of religion, Santa himself is Pagan.

And as you probably know, Christmas was celebrated long before there were any Christians to take up the practice. When the Christians came along and began to celebrate Christmas, they were simply continuing with this age-old festival of Goodwill, although it is possible that their representation of the birth of the Christ Child demonstrated the birth of the energy of Goodwill in a more complete, easy-to-relate to manner than the representations that had come before.

I told myself when I began this document that I was going to try not to cuss, and was going to try to keep my material at a level that could be enjoyed by a general audience, for I realized that some parents would want to share this document with their kids. If you are familiar with some of my other books, you may realize what an unusual approach this is for me. It's so hard not to cuss when writing about the public schools and the denial of Goodwill which they foster.

I will confess to you that I did have to drink a beer.

CHAPTER FOUR: Born Again

It is time for a rebirth of spirituality in the world, and this rebirth will intimately involve the energy of Goodwill, as well as certain other spiritual energies, such as the energy of Synthesis, which allows the total fullness of the energy and experience of Compassion to emerge.

Rituals will emerge that will encourage the presence of these spiritual energies in the lives of those who share their consciousness with one another thru their rituals. If the public schools (and most private schools, too!) are all but useless now, they will be completely useless in this new world, for the new world will encourage the expression of every aspect of ourselves as human beings. Not one iota of the human being will be considered bad or will be neglected, but every aspect of the human being will be encouraged to learn to purify itself of glamour and illusion, and infuse itself with love, as the preparation to joining in that love-inspired Fusion of every aspect of Human Nature that translates as Compassion.

Children will be the masters of these great deeds, as they inspire their elders and one another with their perceptiveness and Creativity. To turn a child loose upon the field of his dreams is to make him the master of his Destiny. He doesn't require restriction; rules, regulations and all that-- oh, that's right, I'm not cussing in this document. What he requires is for his elders to set a tone of Compassionate Discipline by learning to live that Discipline, thus serving as both an example of Compassionate Dream-Building and as a centre of energy that stabilizes the child's own efforts and aspirations. If that sounds hard to understand to you, it's because the public schools taught you to deny your own intelligence in a frenzy of material lust set up by those who are addicted to a materialistic view of science and religion. So you have to recover your own intelligence. You do have it, you'll just have to work hard to recognize and recover it.

And it's important to understand that intelligence results from spiritual strivings toward Love and Compassion. Intelligence developed for its own sake is not true intelligence at all, but is just a delusion used by the smug to deceive themselves and to impress one another in the midst of their stupid deception.

Rules and regulations are related to fate and slavery and stupidity; self-initiated spiritual strivings toward contacting and recognizing Love, then learning to fully embody Love so it translates as Compassion, is the Path to Achieve Destiny. In other words, fate is unconscious, while Destiny is the conscious, creative result of the fully conscious reclamation of every aspect of Human Nature. For Human Nature is the Soul Nature; thus Human Nature is Divine. We do not neglect or abuse or denigrate the body, because the body is an extension of the Soul, and is how all aspects of Soul learn to know themselves and manifest themselves fully in the material dimension. We do not repress the body or the emotions, because these are a part of the Soul Body in the final analysis, and the Soul Body must be allowed to roam free where it can best serve. So we teach our bodies and emotions how they can be fulfilled in a disciplined, wholebody way that is unrestricted and that allows everyone else the same freedom. This is accomplished as we Work diligently to become masters of morality. Morality is not very closely related to most people's ideas of morality, so most people's--including most "moral philosopher's"--ideas on the subject are useless, and even harmful. It takes a disciplined, long-term inquiry to discover that morality is a way of applying energy-- specifically the energy of Love and Compassion--in an efficient manner. Glamour and illusion get in the way of this application, so the practice of learning morality includes as a huge part of its nature learning to release glamour and illusion. All

22

the energy bodies have to be cleared of glamour and illusion for the sacred Human Being, the Child of God, to become a Liberated Human Being, and the proper apprehension of the science of morality is a big necessary step involved in this.

Of course, there are many levels of the process of becoming Liberated, with each major level being marked off by a new application of energy from the Great Deva who rules over our earth. This application of energy is known as Initiation. It is not the type of initiation you might get in a church or fraternal order. This type of energy-application from the Lord of the World is a unique experience that can only be enjoyed in whatever one's unique circumstances are at the time of the application. It is not prefabricated, because each person's spiritual path is so unique. The application of energy from the Lord of the World will flow thru the Human Being in a manner largely dictated by the spiritual channels the Human Being has uncovered within himself thru his own dedicated spiritual strivings.

Santa Claus is intimately connected with the very first initiation, which is usually called the "Birth Initiation". This is the Initiation at which the energy of the soul becomes active in the Human Heart and manifests as Goodwill. Merry Christmas, sweet Christ Child. The birth of Jesus in a barn surrounded by animals symbolized, among other things, the birth of the divine soul-nature into an animal body and consciousness, so that the animal-human begins to become conscious of himself as a Human Being.

In time, this First Initiation will probably become a public event of supreme ritual, as more and more folks prepare themselves for this particular application of energy. This Initiation, which used to be administered only to one candidate at a time (due to the scarcity of candidates!) is now being administered to folks in group formation. In other words, people who resonate to a similar tone group themselves around one another and receive this blessing, this First Initiation, together. So nowadays this Initiation is experienced both as a unique individual pattern by each freshly-made Initiate, and also as a group experience of a larger energy-pattern, a group experience of soulness that resonates thru a great pattern of Creativity for everyone who vibrates to a similar tone.

Man, that's groovey, isn't it?

CHAPTER FIVE: Family Relations

We have spoken of the rituals of putting up the Christmas tree and of leaving out cookies and milk to invoke Santa, thus bringing the energy of Goodwill into our home. And as we do these things within our own family pattern, let us not forget our own household devas and the nature spirits they supervise in the task of keeping the energy pattern of our unique family together. We want to honor and acknowledge their presence as a part of our family and their contributions to our family.

However, we must be careful to relate to the members of the deva evolution in the proper way. For starters, we must remember that we are not the supervisors of the "wee people", the nature spirits that surround us. The "wee people" are supervised by devas--angels--who know exactly how to encourage the "wee people" to occupy the proper place in the pattern at the proper moment. If a human makes the mistake of trying to supervise the "wee people", all sorts of problems can result, including possibly some harm to all involved, whether nature spirit or human person.

Humans can learn to cooperate with the devas thru developing sensitivity to energy. We cooperate with devas, but we let the devas direct the wee folk who serve as the load-shifters within the pattern, moving energies and encouraging events.

Those who should have known better have written that nature spirits are "controlled" by devas, but this is not the case at all. Nature spirits are *directed and encouraged* by devas, not controlled. Maybe this is one reason human beings usually mess things up if they try to interact much with nature spirits. Human beings today are typically control freaks, but there is no such thing as control in the deva-world. The direction that devas enjoy from "greater" devas, and the direction and encouragement that nature spirits enjoy from their supervisory devas, is not experienced as control at all. It must always be remembered that devic consciousness is very different from human consciousness, and we cannot take anything for granted when dealing with the angel evolution. Angels and nature spirits do not experience life in the same way as members of the Human evolution.

So when I say nature spirits are encouraged by devas, I *am not* saying the same thing I would be saying if I said Tom Human encouraged Betty Human. Both the direction and encouragement that occur in the deva world are experienced as energy; one a more direct impulse, the other as a more sustaining impulse with an overtone of slight movement. I realize I may not have succeeded very well at communicating much to your consciousness with the above lines, but we are hampered by the limitations of language. But we have to use language for the time being, so we do the best job we can with the tool we have available. Eventually we will have better tools.

I haven't read very much about devas and nature spirits; most of what I've learned I've had to learn because my karma led me to circumstances in which I've had to become intimately involved with them. In fact, I never actually wanted anything to do with them, but in the end my karma had to fulfill itself by bringing me into a working relationship with them.

Well, the wise Rolling Stones pointed out that "You can't always get what you want" but that if you try "you'll get what you need". How kind of them to point this out. It is good to see my own experience confirmed.

As stated, I haven't read much about the world of devas--which is our world as well; it's just that humans and devas interact with the world differently--but there is one book I can recommend. It is called *WORKING WITH ANGELS, FAIRIES AND NATURE SPIRITS* and was written by an English bloke named William Bloom. This guy has a doctorate in political psychology, but he hasn't let it ruin his life. He has remained open to the natural world, to the spiritual world. The book is neither scholarly nor is it filled with new-age foolishness. It provides a stable platform for viewing the world of the devas and wee people thru your own consciousness. It is only 160 pages long, so do not be afraid of it. You can read it quickly enough and still have time left over for whatever vices you had originally intended to practice.

I am sure there are other good books out there about the deva kingdom, but I haven't read them. I've been too busy trying to adjust my own pattern to devic influences; learning on the job, you know. I am even more sure there are plenty of useless or ridiculous books out there, so be plenty careful. Lots of fools write books, so always trust your own judgement and experience more than you trust anything written in any book, including this one.

There are practical reasons for trusting your own judgement and experience more than anything you read even in a really good book, such as the one you're presently holding in your hands. For example, we've already noted the difficulty of communicating thru the use of language. Misunderstandings, whether slight or great, may easily arise. Perhaps at times I do not make myself as clear as I might; perhaps at other times you are not as attentive a student of my wisdom as you could be. In either case, you might wind up with an unclear idea of what I'm trying to communicate. So trust your own ideas; since you are so heavily invested in your own ideas, you are probably a more attentive student of them than you are of anyone else's ideas, anyway. If not, why not?

Trust yourself, baby.

Over the temple of Apollo at Delphi there was an inscription that said "Know Yourself". That's sound advice. If I ever get a temple in America the inscription will probably read "Trust Yourself". That's the next step.

CHAPTER SIX: Feel The Pattern

Many traditional cultures around the world acknowledged their household supervisor deva each day. Some still do. This acknowledgement may be as simple as lighting a candle first thing in the morning and having a moment of silence. Or it could be more elaborate, depending on what you and the deva work out together. That chap William Bloom can explain how to work with devas better than I can, so go see him.

Each race of humans also has its supervisor deva, the one who holds the pattern which it is the Destiny of that race to consciously fulfill. This pattern is not rigid; it is flowing and graceful and highly structured. You could say it is firm, but firmness and rigidity are definitely not the same thing. Firmness has flexibility built into its very nature; thus the pattern sustains itself for a long, long time. Only that which is both flexible and efficient endures.

When a particular race is founded, One goes forth from the Council Chamber of the Lord of the World and, among other Achievements, finally learns to both create and hold the Pattern for the new race. Just as this One is a reflection of the Lord of the World, the Race-Founder's influence causes, in time, a race to emerge which is reflective of the new nature he earned for Himself.

Each Race-Founder reflects the Lord of the World a little differently and according to some unique new energy-tone, which is why we've wound up with so many different races and subraces. For this process goes on at a variety of intensities, so we find that we not only have seven Races, but that each of these Races has seven subraces, and each subrace has seven family races. That's the general scheme. In an environment such as we live in today in North America, we have the mingling of many different bloodlines from many different races, and in the context of our times, this is a good thing. It means that another Race is about ready to emerge, because for whatever reason, new Races must always carry the blood of several other races that have already been passing thru the cycles of earth-experience for a while.

It is crucial for people to learn to connect with the pattern of their various races. We are at a point in human spiritual evolution (and all genuine evolution *is* spiritual evolution . . . of course, there are physical effects too, but this isn't surprising when you remember that the body is an extension of the Soul) where the Ones who founded the Races see the possibility of the Races learning to live as "good neighbors", but this can only occur if people are conscious of themselves within the context of their own racial pattern. And if you aren't sure what your racial pattern is, your own bloodline will gradually reveal that to you if you learn to listen to your body and blood. Even if you are of mixed blood, your blood will most likely gravitate toward a particular pattern, so go with what feels right to you. If you think about it when you should be *feeling* the little racial patterns in your blood--the little devas in your blood--you are likely to deceive yourself. Feeling our blood always tells us our options and leads us home. Thinking usually misleads us.

CHAPTER SEVEN: Beyond Freud

Psychology will begin to mature when it embraces the Archetypes and the Seven Living Rays of Energy. As you may know, some of the more advanced psychologists are already embracing the Science of the Archetypes, and may be on the verge of embracing the actual Experience of the Archetypes. How healthy that is! This is a mighty first step toward embracing the fullness of our Divine Human Nature. For each Archetype--or God and Goddess, if you prefer that wonderful Pagan lingo--is a Great Deva whose job is to hold the Divine Pattern for some aspect of Human Nature. Each Archetype reflects also the tone of whatever Race or Subrace it is assigned to. For example, the Odin of Scandinavia could be considered roughly equivalent to the Shiva of the Indian subcontinent. And Thor could be considered equivalent to Vishnu.

I have read just a bit about how Thor was considered the Number One God in some regions of Scandinavia rather than Odin. I get the impression there's some puzzlement among some scholars about this. But no puzzle exists except in the minds of scholars, who should be pursuing the truth of their own blood, if they ever expect to arrive at the truth of the Gods or of their own Race.

Thor was considered number one because

the blood of the people told them that Thor was directly concerned with preserving their Racial Pattern and the way of life that flowed from that pattern. Odin was known to the blood of the people as an incarnation of Shiva, and most people are frankly uncomfortable around Shiva. However, what the people may not have recognized is that Shiva precedes Vishnu; Odin precedes Thor. The Destroyer appears and breaks up some old pattern that has become restrictive, or some aspect of a pattern that has become restrictive. Then the Destroyer's self-evolution carries him on the march into crafting a new Pattern, and along the Path of this Craft Odin gradually becomes Thor. Odin undergoes intense and indescribable Processes that translate him into Thor, so that the Destroyer becomes Creator, and then Preserver.

Dig?

The Seven Living Rays of Energy smile upon the planet in various combinations, and touch each human being whether she is aware of it or not according to the combinations that are right for her present incarnation. This is a huge field of investigation and my little tract is not so ambitious as to try to do more than indicate the fact of the Rays. Then if you are interested, maybe your own experience will lead you into greater Discovery. Howdy,

Columbus!

Of course, the Rays also touch the Races. It seems pretty obvious that the forceful, direct Norse have a lot of First Ray in their makeup, because the First Ray is the Ray of Will or Power. It is also called the Ray of Synthesis, because the application of the energy of this Ray is necessary in coordinating all aspects of human experience. But the Second Ray of Love-Wisdom is just as necessary in bringing about Synthesis, and maybe is even more necessary in the long run, because the whole purpose of Synthesis is to allow Love to shine throughout the entire nature of the Human Being. When this is fully accomplished, the Human Being is Liberated from lust and is a walking incarnation of Compassion, a Liberated Human Being. Thus he carries the title Lord of Compassion.

The Orientalists preach freedom from desire, but I think that is a load of crap. (I'm still trying not to cuss, but I don't think the previous sentence could quite be considered cussing.) As long as we are Human we will experience the Divine Energy of Desire, and this is as it should be. Desire is directly associated with Creation, and it is our purpose to join with all of Nature in Creation. Full-Spectrum Desire, across every aspect of Human Nature, is necessary for us to be fully Creative. Duh! This seems obvious. Obvious to everyone but the Orientalists, but the Orientalists are scholars, and scholars are usually deluded by the lusts of the intellect, which is one of the smallest parts of human nature, and which in most people has an inferiority complex which causes it to pretend to be superior and to try to hog the whole show of the person's awareness.

I say that we must purify ourselves of glamour and illusion, releasing these impure elements so we can experience that pure Desire of the Awakened Human Being. In other words, I say we must release lust, not desire. We can't get rid of desire anyway, and if we try, it will secretly sneak around behind our backs and manifest as lust, and will furthermore be a worse, more impure lust than it was before we started trying to get rid of it. So-called spiritual disciplines which preach getting rid of desire were created by either fools or by bad people who wanted to deliberately hurt their neighbors. I had to try really hard not to cuss and call those foolish people names as I wrote that line.

A few more comments on the Rays and I'll let you get back to your Cinemax or whatever it was you really wanted to do.

The Third Ray is the Ray of Active Intelligence. A person with a Third Ray mental body might be pretty smart, but a person with a Third Ray physical body would be smart in a somewhat corresponding way. Since the physical brain is related to the mental body, we see here a condition of "overlap", for want of a better word. I really dig chicks who have Third Ray physical bodies. Their bodies are intelligent in a quick, efficient manner that I find most appealing.

But if you want to know the whole truth, I dig the physical bodies of chicks who inhabit most of the rays. Variety is the spice of life, as they say. Whoever coined that phrase must have had a wholesome, desire-filled relationship with the Seven Rays.

The Fourth Ray is the Ray of Harmony thru Conflict; sometimes I call it the Ray of Coordination, because in my experience, when oscillating with the First Ray, with both these Rays infused by, motivated by and empowered by Love and Compassion, you can get a lot of Work done with respect to Coordinating all levels of Divine-Human experience.

The Fifth Ray is the Ray of Concrete Knowledge, or Science. The Sixth Ray is the Ray of Idealism, and is the Ray that the World Religions of the past two thousand years perverted into fanaticism. It was the predominant influence during the last two millennia, but now it is passing out of active manifestation.

The Seventh Ray is the Ray of Ceremonial Order. Sometimes I call it the Ray of Rhythmic Activity, and It doesn't seem to mind. This is the Ray that governs this new Age of Aquarius, and it has been cycling into manifestation now for over three centuries. Soon it will be the primary Ray in manifestation, and it feels to me as if it already is.

It must always be remembered that *every* Ray is actually Sourced in the Second Ray of Love-Wisdom that governs our Solar System. Each Ray is really meant to lend its own unique tone to the Love-Wisdom which is It's parent as it cycles into manifestation for a term, then yields It's place to one of It's Great Brothers, which then will lend the earth the predominant Tone by which Love-Wisdom is carried throughout the earth.

Well, I hope that's clear enough. As I said, I'm not trying to offer a full treatment of the Rays, just trying to indicate their existence. You can do the rest, honey chile.

CHAPTER EIGHT: Heartlife And Reflections

We've been proving the existence of Santa, and I hope you now are satisfied that He does exist and can be called upon to bless your home with Goodwill. Of course, there are also other Beings who can be called upon for the same purpose, such as the Christ.

For the Goodwill to take hold in your home and in your life, you have to be willing to allow your Heart to open. This can be exciting and exhilarating, and it can also be rather difficult at times. Once your Heart is open, you may encounter challenges that cause you to feel you have to shut your Heart down for a while to protect it, at least until you have learned more about working with the Heart and discovered how to keep it open and protected at the same time.

Misunderstandings arise in human relationships and in those human interactions which don't qualify as relationships. In learning to spread the Goodwill of our Hearts, we have to learn also to take care of our Hearts, because of our own potential to misjudge whether another person is ready to experience our Goodwill, or whether a given person will correctly interpret the Goodwill.

When I first opened my Heart, I wanted to hug everybody, and pretty much did. I was informed by one person that I had a "healing hug". Another person thought I was a sexual deviant, and when I found this out I shut down my Heart and quit hugging people for a while.

Others who have opened their Hearts have had a similar experience. I was told about a lawyer (of all professions!) who had opened his Heart and was in the I-Want-To-Hug-Everyone stage. He hung out at a bakery or some such place on a regular basis . . . until someone complained to the management about his behavior, and management broke his Heart by asking him to stay away from the bakery. I hope the guy eventually managed to forgive everyone involved and recovered his Heart.

When we open our Hearts, we tend to flow over our boundaries. The trick is to learn not to flow over other people's boundaries, too!

Of course, there are those people--those parasites--who deliberately flow over other people's boundaries in order to suck their energy, or to imprint them with some form of perverted lust. Or both. So boundaries are important, and all sincere people must learn to respect other people's boundaries, whether we understand why they have those particular boundaries or not. Plus, we must cultivate our own boundaries, for precisely the reason that parasites exist, and we have to be ready to deal firmly and decisively with them.

When Santa comes, he shows up in an

etheric body if he shows up in a body at all. This means you may not see him, because the etheric body is the energy body that is next up from the physical body in vibrational tone. He can "condense" his etheric body enough for you to see it if he wants, but probably would only do so if you were a disciple of your own Heart's Goodwill. Even then he might not do it, because everything in life takes energy, so if Santa is to use his precious energy in some way, it will be in the way he deems most appropriate at that particular moment. It is very important for all of us to learn to use energy efficiently, so it is a good idea for all of us to follow Santa's example in this matter.

Sometimes Santa may appear as a whistling wind, possibly without any body at all. But if you feel Goodwill on the air, you know Santa is near.

Santa and other devas and nature spirits often appear as flashes of light. You probably have seen such flashes yourself from time to time, because nature spirits aren't an endangered species, they are everywhere.

They speak the language of metaphor, not the language of the textbooks written by literal-brained scholars. Devas and nature spirits reflect images from out of your own consciousness back upon you; the trick is to recognize the energy of the being's Heart, if that is possible for you at this time, and of the general vibrational tone of the being. Learning to correctly interpret the symbols from out of your own consciousness which are revealed to you by the deva or nature spirit, and marrying that understanding to your sensitivity to the energy the little being is emitting, will help you to understand the message of the being. This is true whether you are awake or asleep; remember that many times your dreams are communications with the kingdom of the devas and nature spirits.

Last night, for example, I dreamed of a suitcase with a particular mountain painted on it. Well, I've been wanting to move back out West for quite some time, and that particular mountain is almost as far West as you can go on this continent. So it is pretty obvious that this is a hopeful sign that I will be able to ramble in the land of my dreams before long.

Also, I dreamed of a woman I knew when I lived out West who was a talented energy-healer. The woman in the dream may not have been this woman at all; it could easily have been a deva impersonating that woman in order to convey to me that my own healing is about to be far enough along for me to ramble in the land of my dreams.

During an interview a well-known singer talked about how sometimes women stop him on the street and tell him that they knew he was in the room when they were listening to his music and being intimate with their husbands. He would protest and say, "No, I wasn't there," but these women would insist that he had been there. Well, ladies, I can tell you who was there: a deva was there! And this deva was reflecting the mood and image you had of the singer back upon you, because this is what devas do.

CHAPTER NINE: A New Set of Duds

When we are involved in Healing Work, a big part of that process involves releasing old energies that no longer serve us. Devas sort of put these energies on like an old coat and prance around in them while we are feeling them--because we have to feel them to release them--and as the energy-release is winding down, the devas themselves then release these old "clothes" and they disappear into thin air. This is a part of the healing process. This is how we trade in old garments so we can dress ourselves up in shiny new garments.

Thoreau is famous for having said that people should be wary of any enterprise that requires new clothes, but Thoreau was all mixed-up. Everyone must go thru the healing, cleansing process at some point, and it usually takes a long time to accomplish genuinely deep healing work. And during this work, you "clean out your closet", constantly trading old clothes for shiny new clothes. You exist in so many different dimensions which you may not currently be aware of that you require a lot of clothes. You will start to become aware of some of these dimensions during deep healing Work.

Human Beings are legendary figures, just as legendary as the devas and elves and other nature spirits we work with. And legendary figures dress in certain ways, and match their garments to the particular plane of livingness on which they find themselves at any given moment. I knew a woman who was saved from a terrible car accident. The spirit who assisted in her salvation appeared dressed as a police officer and comforted her a bit until the humans arrived, at which point he disappeared. I knew another woman who was saved--just barely--from a terrible accident, but her salvation was accomplished by a group of humans who work from the etheric dimension and whom I think of as the "Orange Berets", because in my experience this group wears orange berets. Or at least they used to; I haven't been in touch with them for some years and it wouldn't surprise me if they've changed their uniform by now to match changing planetary frequencies. I'll bet they have.

Constantly upgrading the wardrobe is a way of life for the Evolutionary. I guess this is a statement the chicks will be able to relate to. But what the chicks have to learn is that when they get new shoes, it often must involve throwing away the old ones!

Efficiency depends on releasing the old as we accept the new . . . not on repressing the old, but on *releasing* the old. As long as we do our part and are really willing to release those old, stale energies as they come up, the devas involved in such theatricality will show up to wear the clothes for a few minutes during the release process so you can have some idea what you're releasing. And you must be willing to let it go for it to go. Performing an inquiry into the nature of nonattachment might be helpful. I will give you this important hint: many of the people who preach nonattachment are attached to hot air and don't know what they are talking about. They appear to be trying to detach themselves from their humanity and normal human emotions. That's not the way to go, baby. You don't want to become a mechanical subhuman, you want to become a juicy superhuman who is filled with Compassion for all Beings. This means you have to fully recover your ability to *feel*, not deny your precious feelings. Your feelings can both be indicators of what's wrong and what's right, of what needs to be released and of what needs to be embraced. Your feelings, once you've recovered them, are far less likely to confuse you than your rational mind.

The "rational mind" itself is illogical, because in so many of us it tries to dominate other faculties which are more closely allied to reality. To be healed, it must accept its role as co-creator with the other faculties, not as prince of the other faculties, because in truth, it is not a prince, it is a mechanic with a monkey wrench. However, when it does release the illusions its unstable house of inferiority and superiority are built upon, it finds itself transmuted into a reflector of Compassion and its monkey wrench has suddenly turned to gold.

I've talked enough and I know you hear your favorite vices calling you, so I'll let you go. It is time for me to release the compulsion to speak without regard to whether you want to listen to me or not.

Goodbye. Or perhaps I should say:

MERRY CHRISTMAS!

www.ingramcontent.com/pod-product-compliance
Lightning Source LLC
Chambersburg PA
CBHW061757040426
42447CB00011B/2340